The Early Church Today Series

ST. GREGORY OF NYSSA

THE LIFE OF
ST. MACRINA

THE EARLY CHURCH TODAY SERIES

Volume 6

The early leaders of the Church, tasked with shepherding Christ's flock, left us spiritual wealth that is too often neglected in modern times. The Early Church Today Series, published by the St. Mary & St. Moses Abbey Press, aims to help make that richness more accessible to readers, inviting them to see the applicability of the early Church to our walk with God today. By sharing practical selections from the writings of the early Church, aided by meaningful editorial supplements and revisions, each book will attempt to diminish impediments and bring to light what the Church has to offer.

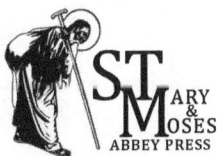

ST MARY & MOSES ABBEY PRESS

THE LIFE OF
ST. MACRINA

ST. GREGORY OF NYSSA

Translation by

W.K. Lowther Clarke

ST
Mary & Moses
ABBEY PRESS

The Life of St. Macrina

By St. Gregory of Nyssa

Translation by W.K. Lowther Clarke

Minor editing of the original translation was done by St. Mary and St. Moses Abbey, mainly changing archaic words to their modern counterparts.

Designed & Published by:
St. Mary & St. Moses Abbey Press
101 S Vista Dr, Sandia, TX 78383
stmabbeypress.com

All Scripture quotations in the footnotes of this book, unless otherwise indicated, are taken from the New King James Version® Copyright © 1982 by Thomas Nelson, Inc. Used by permission. All rights reserved.

Cover Icon of St. Macrina was written by Dalia Sobhi.

CONTENTS

INTRODUCTION

The Life of Gregory of Nyssa

Readers to whom the subject is unfamiliar, should be quite clear in their minds from the outset as to the distinction between the three Gregories who played an important part in the Church history of Asia Minor.

Gregory Thaumaturgus (i.e. "Worker of Wonders") was born of heathen parents at Neo-Caesarea in Pontus; having gone to Palestine for his education, he came under the influence of Origen, then living at Caesarea, and was converted to Christianity. He became bishop of his native city in AD 240, and carried out the work of evangelizing the district most thoroughly. Basil, brother of Gregory of Nyssa, was brought up on the family estate at Annesi, near Neo-Caesarea by his grandmother Macrina, who used to repeat to him the very words used by Gregory Thaumaturgus. Gregory of Nyssa wrote the life of Gregory Thaumaturgus, and to the latter's influence may be ascribed the strong element of Origen-ism in his writings. Through the same channel Origen's teaching reached Basil and Gregory of Nazianzus, who during their stay at their monastery in Pontus compiled the *Philocalia*, or collection of choice passages from Origen.

Gregory of Nazianzus was the friend and contemporary of Basil at the University of Athens, in the pioneer monastery in Pontus, and later on as brother bishop. Soon after Basil became bishop of Caesarea in Cappadocia in AD 370 he forced his friend to accept the see of Sasima, a dusty village where the post changed horses. In AD 379 he went to Constantinople as orthodox bishop; his sermons preached there have become famous. He died about AD 390.

Gregory of Nyssa was the younger brother of Basil and author of the present book. A brief sketch of his life must now be given.

He came of a race of landed proprietors, who had estates in Cappadocia and Pontus and had won honorable distinction by their steadfast devotion to the faith under persecution. His parents, Basil and Emmelia, had ten children, of whom four sons and five daughters survived infancy. The eldest child, Macrina, is the subject of this biography; the other four daughters all made satisfactory marriages. St. Basil the Great was the eldest son. Next to him came Naucratius, who was killed on a hunting expedition in Pontus. Gregory and Peter, the two youngest sons, became bishops eventually of Nyssa and Sebaste. It would be difficult to find in the whole of church history a family so uniformly brilliant.

Gregory was born about AD 335, probably at Caesarea. Apparently he showed no special promise as a boy, nor did he share Basil's educational advantages. It is mentioned in this book, where Macrina, speaking of his fame says: "You that have little or no equipment within yourself for such success." His first serious religious impressions seem to have dated from a service at the chapel of the Forty Martyrs. As he slept in an arbour near the chapel he dreamed that the martyrs beat him with rods. When he awoke, he was filled with remorse, and soon afterwards became a Reader. But presently, much to the disgust of Gregory of Nazianzus, he deserted his post in order to become a professor of rhetoric.

About this time he married a lady named Theosebia, if this is the true interpretation of some difficult passages. But his growing seriousness, and the example of his brothers and sister, led him before long to espouse the ascetic life and become a member of the monastery in Pontus, where he spent some quiet and studious years. Indeed, he was by nature far better fitted to be a student than a man of affairs. A striking example of the simplicity of his character is afforded by the methods he adopted in order to heal a quarrel between his brother Basil and their uncle Gregory. He actually forged a letter purporting to come from the latter and asking for a reconciliation. In Basil's 58th Epistle may be read the crushing rebuke administered by the elder brother.

In AD 370 Basil had become bishop and metropolitan of Caesarea. He found the post one of great difficulty, especially in view of the opposition of some of his suffragans. In AD 372, wishing to strengthen his position by surrounding himself with men whom he could trust, he forced his friend Gregory to accept the bishopric of Sasima, and his brother that of Nyssa. We need not recount in detail the troubles that pursued Gregory during the episcopate. He was deposed and banished in AD 376, but was recalled on the death of the Emperor Valens in AD 378.

On January 1, AD 379, Basil died; in September of the same year Gregory attended a Council at Antioch, after which he determined to visit his sister Macrina in the monastery of Annesi. The visit is described at length in the present book. When the funeral ceremonies were over, he returned to his diocese, only to find a sad state of confusion. Having introduced a certain measure of order, he set out on his travels once more, and visited Babylon with a view of reforming the Church there. After this he went to the holy places of Palestine, where nothing but disillusionment awaited him. In AD 381 he was present at the Council of Constantinople, and on several subsequent occasions we find him at that city. His death occurred about AD 395.

Gregory of Nyssa is a figure of great importance in the history of Christian doctrine and the eventual triumph of Nicene orthodoxy.

THE LIFE OF ST. MACRINA

[To the Monk Olympus]

Introduction

The form of this volume, if one may judge from its heading, is apparently epistolary, but its bulk exceeds that of a letter, extending as it does to the length of a book. My apology must be that the subject on which you bade me write is greater than can be compressed within the limits of a letter.

I am sure you do not forget our meeting, when, on my way to Jerusalem in pursuance of a vow, in order to see the relics of the Lord's sojourning in the flesh on the actual spots, I ran across you in the city of Antioch; and you must remember all the different talks we enjoyed, for it was not likely that our meeting would be a silent one, when your wit provided so many subjects for conversation. As often happens at such times, the talk flowed on until we came to discuss the life of some famous person. In this case it was a woman who provided us with our subject; if indeed she should be styled woman, for I do not know whether it is fitting to designate her by her sex, who so surpassed her sex. Our account of her was not based on the narrative of others, but our talk was an accurate description of what we had learned by personal experience, nor did it need to be authenticated by strangers. Nor even was the virgin referred to unknown to our family circle, to make it necessary to learn the wonders of her life through others, but she came from the same parents as ourselves, being, so to speak, an offering of first-fruits, since she was the earliest born of my mother's womb. As then you have decided that the story of her noble career is worth telling, to prevent such a life being unknown to our time, and the record of a woman who raised herself by "philosophy"[1] to the greatest height of human virtue passing into the shades of useless oblivion, I thought it well to obey you, and in a few words, as best I can, to tell her story in unstudied and simple style.

Macrina's Parents

The virgin's name was Macrina; she was so called by her parents after a famous Macrina some time before in the family, our father's mother, who had confessed Christ like a good athlete in the time of persecutions. This indeed was her name to the outside world, the one used by her friends. But another name had been given her privately, as the result of a vision before she was born into the world. For indeed her mother

---

1   The use of the word "philosophy" to designate Christianity is common in the writings of the fourth century, and may perhaps be traced back to Origen's synthesis of the Gospel and philosophy. It is employed in a twofold sense, of the Christian religion generally and of asceticism in particular. Cf. Gregory Nazianzus, *Oration VII*, 9 (describing the asceticism of his brother Caesarius): "As philosophy is the greatest so is it the most difficult, of professions, which can be taken in hand by few, and only by those who have been called forth by the divine magnanimity."

was so virtuous that she was guided on all occasions by the divine will. In particular she loved the pure and unstained mode of life so much that she was unwilling to be married. But since she had lost both her parents, and was in the very flower of her youthful beauty, and the fame of her good looks was attracting many suitors, and there was a danger that, if she were not mated to some one willingly, she might suffer some unwished-for violent fate, seeing that some men, inflamed by her beauty, were ready to abduct her—on this account she chose for her a husband a man who was known and approved for the gravity of his conduct, and so gained a protector of her life.

The Birth of Macrina

At her first confinement she became the mother of Macrina. When the due time came for her pangs to be ended by delivery, she fell asleep and seemed to be carrying in her hands that which was still in her womb. And some one in form and raiment more splendid than a human being appeared and addressed the child she was carrying by the name of Thecla, that Thecla, I mean, who is so famous among the virgins.[2] After doing this and testifying to it three times, he departed from her sight and gave her an easy delivery, so that at that moment she awoke from her sleep and saw her dream realized.

---

2   Thecla was a contemporary of St. Paul.

15

Now this name was used only in secret. But it seems to me that the apparition spoke not so much to guide the mother to a right choice of a name, as to forecast the life of the young child, and to indicate by the name that she would follow her namesake's mode of life.

Macrina's Childhood

Well, the child was reared. Although she had her own nurse, yet as a rule her mother did the nursing with her own hands. After passing the stage of infancy, she showed herself apt in acquiring childish accomplishments, and her natural powers were shown in every study to which her parents' judgement directed her. The education of the child was her mother's task; she did not, however, employ the usual worldly method of education, which makes a practice of using poetry as a means of training the early years of the child. For she considered it disgraceful and quite unsuitable, that a tender and plastic nature should be taught either those tragic passions of womanhood which afforded poets their suggestions and plots, or the indecencies of comedy, to be, so to speak, defiled with unseemly tales of "the harem." But such parts of inspired Scripture as you would think were incomprehensible to young children were the subject of the girl's studies; in particular the Wisdom of Solomon, and those parts of it especially which have an ethical bearing. Nor was she ignorant of any part of the Psalter, but at stated times she recited every part of it. When she rose from bed, or engaged in household duties, or rested, or partook of food, or retired from table, when she went to bed or rose in the night for prayer, the Psalter was her constant companion, like a good fellow-traveler that never deserted her.

Her Betrothal

Filling her time with these and the like occupations, and attaining besides a considerable proficiency in wool-work, the growing girl reached her twelfth year, the age when the bloom of adolescence begins to appear. In which connection it is noteworthy that the girl's beauty could not be concealed in spite of efforts to hide it. Nor in all the countryside so it seems, was there anything so marvelous as her beauty in comparison with that of others. So fair was she that even painters' hands could not do justice to her comeliness; the art that contrives all things and essays the greatest tasks, so as even to model in imitation the figures of the heavenly bodies, could not accurately reproduce the loveliness of her form. In consequence a great swarm of suitors seeking her in marriage crowded round her parents. But her father—a shrewd man with a reputation for forming right decisions—picked our from the rest a young man related to the family, who was just leaving school, of good birth and remarkable steadiness, and decided to betroth his daughter to him, as soon as she was old enough. Meantime he aroused great hopes, and he offered to his future father-in-law his fame in public speaking, as it were one of the bridegroom's gifts; for he displayed the power of his eloquence in forensic contests on behalf of the wronged.

Death of the Young Man

But Envy cut off these bright hopes by snatching away the poor lad from life. Now Macrina was not ignorant of her father's schemes. But when the plan formed for her was shattered by the young man's death, she said her father's intention was equivalent to a marriage, and resolved to remain single henceforward, just as if the intention had become accomplished fact. And indeed her determination was more steadfast than could have been expected from her age. For when her parents brought proposals of marriage to her, as often happened owing to the number of suitors that came attracted by the fame of her beauty, she would say that it was absurd and unlawful not to be faithful to the marriage that had been arranged for her by her father, but to be compelled to consider another; since in the nature of things there was but one marriage, as there is one birth and one death. She persisted that the man who had been linked to her by her parents' agreement was not dead, but that she considered him who lived to God, thanks to the hope of the resurrection, to be absent only, not dead; it was wrong not to keep faith with the bridegroom who was away.

Macrina Resolves Never to Leave Her Mother

With such words repelling those who tried to talk her over, she settled on one safeguard of her good resolution, in a resolve not to be separated from her mother even for a moment of time. So that her mother would often say that she had carried the rest of her children in her womb for a definite time, but that Macrina she bore always, since in a sense she ever carried her about. But the daughter's companionship was not a burden to her mother, nor profitless. For the attentions received from her daughter were worth those of many maidservants, and the benefits were mutual. For the mother looked after the girl's soul, and the girl looked after the mother's body, and in all respects fulfilled the required services, even going so far as to prepare meals for her mother with her own hands. Not that she made this her chief business. But after she had anointed her hands by the performance of religious duties—for she deemed that zeal for this was consistent with the principles of her life—in the time that was left she prepared food for her mother by her own toil. And not only this, but she helped her mother to bear her burden of responsibilities. For she had four sons and five daughters, and paid taxes to three different governors, since her property was scattered in as many districts. In consequence her mother was distracted with various anxieties, for her

19

father had by this time departed this life. In all these matters she shared her mother's toils, dividing her cares with her, and lightening her heavy load of sorrows. At one and the same time, thanks to her mother's guardianship, she was keeping her own life blameless, so that her mother's eye both directed and witnessed all she did; and also by her own life she instructed her mother greatly, leading her to the same mark, that of philosophy I mean, and gradually drawing her on to the immaterial and more perfect life.

Basil Returns From the University

When the mother had arranged excellent marriages for the other sisters, such as was best in each case, Macrina's brother, the great Basil, returned after his long period of education, already a practiced rhetorician. He was puffed up beyond measure with the pride of oratory and looked down on the local dignitaries, excelling in his own estimation all the men of leading and position. Nevertheless Macrina took him in hand, and with such speed did she draw him also toward the mark of philosophy that he forsook the glories of this world and despised fame gained by speaking, and deserted it for this busy life where one toils with one's hands. His renunciation of property was complete, lest anything should impede the life of virtue. But, indeed, his life and the subsequent acts, by which he became renowned throughout the world and put into the shade all those who have won renown for their virtue, would need a long description and much time. But I must divert my tale to its appointed task.

Now that all the distractions of the material life had been removed, Macrina persuaded her mother to give up her ordinary life and all showy style of living and the services of domestics to which she had been accustomed before, and bring her point of view down to that of the masses, and to share the life of the maids, treating all her slave girls and menials as if they were sisters and belonged to the same rank as herself.

But at this point I should like to insert a short parenthesis in my narrative and not to pass over unrelated such a matter as the following, in which the lofty character of the maiden is displayed.

The Story of Naucratius

The second of our four brothers, Naucratius, by name, who came next after the great Basil, excelled the rest in natural endowments and physical beauty, in strength, speed, and ability to turn his hand to anything. When he had reached his twenty-first year, and had given such demonstration of his studies by speaking in public, that the whole audience in the theatre was thrilled, he was led by a divine providence to despise all that was already in his grasp, and drawn by an irresistible impulse went off to a life of solitude and poverty. He took nothing with him but himself, save that one of the servants named Chrysapius followed him, because of the affection he had towards his master and the intention he had formed to lead the same life. So he lived by himself, having found a solitary spot on the banks of the Iris—a river flowing through the midst of Pontus. It

21

rises actually in Armenia, passes through our parts, and discharges its stream into the Black Sea. By it the young man found a place with luxuriant growth of trees and a hill nestling under the mass of the over hanging mountain. There he lived far removed from the noises of the city and the distractions that surround the lives both of the soldier and the pleader in the law courts. Having thus freed himself from the din of cares that impedes man's higher life, with his own hands he looked after some old people who were living in poverty and feebleness, considering it appropriate to his mode of life to make such a work in his care. So the generous youth would go on fishing expeditions, and since he was expert in every form of sport, he provided food to his grateful clients by this means. And at the same time by such exercises he was taming his own manhood. Besides this, he also gladly obeyed his mother's wishes whenever she issued a command. And so in these two ways he guided his life, subduing his youthful nature by toils and caring assiduously for his mother, and thus keeping the divine commands he was traveling home to God.

In this manner he completed the fifth year of his life as a philosopher, by which he made his mother happy, both by the way in which he adorned his own life by continence, and by the devotion of all his powers to do the will of her that bore him.

The Tragic Death of Naucratius

Then there fell on the mother a grievous and tragic affliction, contrived, I think, by the Adversary, which brought trouble and mourning upon all the family. For he was snatched suddenly away from life. No previous sickness had prepared them for the blow, nor did any of the usual and well-known mischances bring death upon the young man. Having started out on one of the expeditions, by which he provided necessaries for the old men under his care, he was brought back home dead, together with Chrysapius who shared his life. His mother was far away, three days distant from the scene of the tragedy. Some one came to her telling the bad news. Perfect though she was in every department of virtue, yet nature dominated her as it does others. For she collapsed, and in a moment lost both breath and speech, and she was thrown to the ground by the assault of the evil tidings, like some noble athlete hit by an unexpected blow.

Macrina the One Support of Her Mother

And now the virtue of the great Macrina was displayed. Facing the disaster in a rational spirit, she both preserved herself from collapse, and becoming the prop of her mother's weakness, raised her up from the abyss of grief, and by her own steadfastness and imperturbability taught her mother's soul to be brave. In consequence, her mother was not overwhelmed by the affliction, nor did she behave in any ignoble and womanish way, so as to cry out at the calamity, or tear her dress, or lament over the trouble or strike up funeral chants with mournful melodies. On the contrary she resisted the impulses of nature, and quieted herself both by such reflections as occurred to her spontaneously, and those that were applied by her daughter to cure the ill. For then was the nobility of Macrina's soul most of all conspicuous; since natural affection was making her suffer as well. For it was a brother, and a favorite brother, who had been snatched away by such a manner of death. Nevertheless, conquering nature, she so sustained her mother by her arguments that she, too, rose superior to her sorrow. Besides which, the moral elevation always maintained by Macrina's life gave her mother the opportunity of rejoicing over the blessings she enjoyed rather than grieving over those that were missing.

Mother and Daughter Make Further Progress in the Ascetic Life

When the cares of bringing up and family and the anxieties of their education and settling in life had come to an end, and the property—a frequent cause of worldliness—had been for the most part divided among the children, then, as I said above, the life of the virgin became her mother's guide and led her on to this philosophic and spiritual manner of life. And weaning her from all accustomed luxuries, Macrina drew her on to adopt her own standard of humility. She induced her to live on a footing of equality with the staff of maids, so as to share with them in the same food, the same kind of bed, and in all the necessaries of life, without any regard to differences of rank. Such was the manner of their life, so great the height of their philosophy, and so holy their conduct day and night, as to make the verbal description inadequate. For just as souls freed form the body by death are saved from the cares of this life, so was their life far removed from all earthly follies and ordered with a view of imitating the angelic life. For no anger of jealousy, no hatred or pride, was observed in their midst, nor anything else of this nature, since they had cast away all vain desires for honor and glory, all vanity, arrogance, and the like. Continence was their luxury, and obscurity their glory. Poverty, and the casting away of all material superfluities like dust from their bodies, was their wealth. In fact, of all the things after which men eagerly pursue in this life, there were none with which they could not easily dispense. Nothing was left but the care of divine things and the unceasing round of prayer and endless hymnody, co-extensive with time itself, practiced by night and day. So that to them this meant work, and work so called was rest. What human words could make you realize such a life as this, a life on the borderline between human and spiritual nature? For that nature should be free from human weaknesses is more than can be expected from mankind. But these women fell short of the angelic and immaterial nature only in so far as they appeared in bodily form, and were contained within a human frame, and were dependent upon the organs of sense. Perhaps some might even dare to say that the difference was not to their disadvantage. Since living in the body and yet after the likeness of the immaterial beings, they were not bowed down by the weight of the body but their life was exalted to the skies and they walked on high in company with the powers of heaven.

The period covered by this mode of life was no short

one, and with the lapse of time their successes increased, as their philosophy continually grew purer with the discovery of new blessings.

Peter, the Youngest Brother

Macrina was helped most of all in achieving this great aim of her life by her own brother Peter. With him the mother's pangs ceased, for he was the latest born of the family. At one and the same time he received the names of son and orphan, for as he entered this life his father passed away from it. But the eldest of the family, the subject of our story, took him soon after birth from the nurse's breast and reared him herself and educated him on a lofty system of training, practicing him from infancy in holy studies, so as not to give his soul leisure to turn to vain things.

Thus having become all things to the lad—father, teacher, tutor, mother, giver of all good advice—she produced such results that before the age of boyhood had passed, when he was yet a stripling in the first bloom of tender youth, he aspired to the high mark of philosophy. And, thanks to his natural endowments, he was clever in every art that involves hand-work, so that without any guidance he achieved a completely accurate knowledge of everything that ordinary people learn by time and trouble. Scorning to occupy his time with worldly studies, and having in nature a sufficient instructor in all good knowledge, and always looking to his sister as the model of all good, he advanced to such a height of virtue that in his subsequent life he seemed in no whit inferior to the great Basil. But at this time he was all in all to his sister and mother, co-operating with them in the pursuit of the angelic life. Once when a severe famine had occurred and crowds from all quarters were frequenting the retreat where they lived, drawn by the fame of their benevolence, Peter's kindness supplied such an abundance of food that the desert seemed a city by reason of the number of visitors.

Death of the Mother

It was about this time that the mother died, honored by all, and went to God, yielding up her life in the arms of her two children. It is worth while to give the words of blessing which she used over her children, mentioning each of the absent ones in loving remembrance, so that no single one was deprived of the blessing, and commending especially to God in her prayers those who were present with her.

For as these two sat by her on each side of the bed, she touched them with her hands, and uttered these prayers to God with her dying words—

"To You, O Lord, I give the fruit of my womb as both the first-fruits and tenths. For this my eldest is the first-fruits and this my last born is the tenth. Each is sanctified to You by the Law and they are votive offerings to You. Therefore let Your sanctification descend on this my first and this my tenth."

As she spoke she indicated by gestures her daughter and son. Then, having ceased to bless, she ceased to live, having first bidden her children lay her body in their father's grave. But they, having fulfilled the command, cleaved to philosophy with still loftier resolve, even striving against their own life and eclipsing their previous record by their subsequent successes.

Basil Dies After a Noble Career

Meanwhile Basil, the famous saint, had been elected bishop of the great church of Caesarea. He advanced Peter to the sacred order of the priesthood, consecrating him in person with mystical ceremonial. And in this way a further advance in the direction of dignity and sanctity was made in their life, now that philosophy was enriched by the priesthood.

Eight years after this, the world-renowned Basil departed from men to live with God, to the common grief of his native land and the whole world. Now when Macrina heard the news of the calamity in her distant retreat, she was distressed indeed in soul at so great a loss—for how could she not be distressed at a calamity, which was felt even by the enemies of the truth?—but just as they say that the testing of gold takes place in several furnaces, so that if any impurity escapes the first furnace, it may be separated in the second, and again in the last one all admixture of dross may be purged away—consequently it is the most accurate testing of pure gold if having gone through every furnace it shows no refuse. So it happened also in her case. When her noble character had been tested by these different accessions of trouble, in every respect the metal of her soul was proved to be unadultered and undefiled. The first test was the loss of the one brother, the second the parting from her mother, the third was when the common glory of the family, great Basil, was removed from human life. So she remained, like an invincible athlete in no wise unbroken by the assault of troubles.

Gregory Resolves to Visit His Sister

It was the ninth month or a little longer after this disaster, and a synod of bishops was gathered at Antioch, in which we also took part. And when we broke up, each to go home before the year was over, then I, Gregory, felt a desire to visit Macrina. For a long time had elapsed during which visits were prevented by the distraction of the troubles which I underwent, being constantly driven out from my own country by the leaders of heresy. And when I came to reckon the intervening time during which the troubles had prevented us meeting face to face, no less than eight years, or very nearly that period, seemed to have elapsed.

Now when I had accomplished most of the journey and was one day's journey distant, a vision appeared to me in a dream and filled me with anxious anticipations of the future. I seemed to be carrying martyrs' relics in my hands; a light came from them, such as comes from a clear mirror when it is put facing the sun, so that my eyes were blinded by the brilliance of the rays. The same vision recurred three times that night. I could not clearly understand the riddle of the dream, but I saw trouble for my soul, and I watched carefully so as to judge the vision by events.

When I approached the retreat in which Macrina led

29

her angelic and heavenly life, first of all I asked one of the servants about my brother, whether he were at home. He told us that he had gone out four days ago now, and I understood, which indeed was the case, that he had gone to meet us another way. Then I asked after the great lady. He said she was very ill and I was the more eager to hurry on and complete the remainder of the journey, for a certain anxiety and premonitory fear of what was coming stole in and disquieted me.

Gregory Comes to the Monastery and Finds Macrina on Her Death Bed

But when I came to the actual place, rumor had already announced my arrival to the brotherhood. Then the whole company of the men came streaming out to meet us from their apartments. For it was their custom to honor friends by meeting them. But the band of virgins on the women's side modestly waited in the church for us to arrive. But when the prayers and the blessing was over, and the women, after reverently inclining their head for the blessing, retired to their own apartments, none of them were left with us. I guessed the explanation, that the abbess was not with them. A man led me to the house in which was my great sister, and opened the door. Then I entered that holy dwelling. I found her already terribly afflicted with weakness. She was lying not on a bed or couch, but on the floor; a sack had been spread on a board, and another board propped up her head, so contrived as to act as a pillow, supporting the sinews of the neck in slanting fashion, and holding up the neck comfortably. Now when she saw me near the door she raised herself on her elbow but could not come to meet me, her strength being already drained by fever. But by putting her hands on the floor and leaning over from the pallet as far as she could, she showed the respect due to my rank. I ran to her and embraced her prostrate form, and raising her, again restored her to her usual position. Then she lifted her hand to God and said—

"This favor also You have granted me, O God, and have not deprived me of my desire, because You have stirred up Your servant to visit Your handmaid."

Lest she should vex my soul she stilled her groans and made great efforts to hide, if possible, the difficulty of her breathing. And in every way she tried to be cheerful, both taking the lead herself in friendly talk, and giving us an opportunity by asking questions. When in the course of conversation mention was made of the great Basil, my soul was saddened and my face fell dejectedly. But so far was she from sharing in my affliction that, treating the mention of the saint as an occasion for yet loftier philosophy, she discussed various subjects, inquiring about human affairs and revealing in her conversation the divine purpose concealed in disasters. Besides this, she discussed the future life[3] as if inspired by the Holy Spirit, so that it almost seemed as if my soul were lifted by the help of her words away from mortal nature and placed within the heavenly sanctuary. And just as we learn in the story of

---

3   In the long dialogue *On the Soul and the Resurrection*, St. Gregory purports to reproduce this conversation.

Job that the saint was tormented in every part of his body with discharges owing to the corruption of his wounds, yet did not allow the pain to affect his reasoning power, but in spite of the pains in the body did not relax his activities nor interrupt the lofty sentiments of his discourse—similarly did I see in the case of this great woman. Fever was drying up her strength and driving her on to death, yet she refreshed her body as it were with dew, and thus kept her mind unimpeded in the contemplation of heavenly things, in no way injured by her terrible weakness. And if my narrative were not extending to an unconscionable length I would tell everything in order, how she was uplifted as she discoursed to us on the nature of the soul and explained the reason of life in the flesh, and why man was made, and how he was mortal, and the origin of death and the nature of the journey from death to life again. In all of which she told her tale clearly and consecutively as if inspired by the power of the Holy Spirit, and the even flow of her language was like a fountain whose water streams down uninterruptedly.

She Sends Gregory Away to Rest Himself

When our conversation was finished, she said—

"It is time, brother, for you to rest your body awhile, since it is wearing with the great toil of your journey."

And though I found it a great and genuine rest to see her and hear her noble words, yet since she wanted it so much, that I might in every particular seem to obey my mistress, I found a pretty arbor prepared for me in one of the neighboring gardens, and rested under the shade of the trailing vines. But it was impossible to have any feelings of enjoyment when my soul within me was constrained by gloomy anticipations, for the secret of the vision of my dream seemed to be now revealed to me by what I had seen.

For the image I had seen was indeed true—the relics of a holy martyr which had been dead in sin, but now were resplendent with the indwelling power of the Spirit. I explained this to one of those who had heard me tell the dream before.

We were, as one might guess, in a dejected state, expecting sad tidings, when Macrina, somehow or other divining our condition of mind, sent to us a messenger with more cheerful news, and bade us be of good cheer and have better hope for her, for she was feeling a change for the better. Now this was not said to deceive, but the message was actually true, though we did not know it at the time. For in very truth, just as a runner who has passed his adversary and already drawn near to the end of the stadium, as he approaches the judge's seat and sees the crown of victory, rejoices inwardly as if he had already attained his object, and announces his victory to his sympathizers among the spectators—in such a frame of mind did she, too, tell us to cherish better hopes for her, for she was already looking to the prize of her heavenly calling, and all but uttering the apostle's words: "Henceforward is laid up for me the crown of righteousness, which the righteous Judge shall give me," for "I have fought the good fight, I have finished the course, I have kept the faith."

Accordingly, feeling happy at the good news, we began to enjoy the sights that lay before us. For they were very varied and the arrangements gave much pleasure, since the great lady was careful even of these trifles.

Gregory Returns to Macrina, Who Recalls the Events of Her Childhood

But when we saw her again, for she did not allow us to spend time by ourselves in idleness, she began to recall her past life, beginning with childhood, and describing it all in order as in a history. She recounted as much as she could remember of the life of our parents, and the events that took place both before and after my birth. But her aim throughout was gratitude towards God, for she described our parents' life not so much from the point of view of the reputation they enjoyed in the eyes of contemporaries on account of their riches, as an example of the divine blessing.

My father's parents had their goods confiscated for confessing Christ. Our maternal grandfather was slain by the imperial wrath, and all his possessions were transferred to other masters. Nevertheless their life abounded so in faith that no one was named above them in those times. And moreover, after their substance had been divided into nine parts according to the number of the children, the share of each was so increased by God's blessing, that the income of each of the children exceeded the prosperity of the parents. But when it came to Macrina herself she kept nothing of the things assigned to her in the equal division between brothers and sisters, but all her share was given into the priests' hands according to the divine command. Moreover her life became such by God's help that her hands never ceased to work according to the commandment. Never did she even look for help to any human being, nor did human charity give her the opportunity of a comfortable existence. Never were petitioners turned away, yet never did she appeal for help, but God secretly blessed the little seeds of her good works till they grew into a mighty fruit.

As I told my own trouble and all that I had been through, first my exile at the hands of the Emperor Valens on account of the faith, and then the confusion in the Church that summoned me to conflicts and trials, my great sister said—

"Will you not cease to be insensible to the divine blessings? Will you not remedy the ingratitude of your soul? Will you not compare your position with that of your parents'? And yet, as regards worldly things, we make our boast of being well born and thinking we come of a noble family. Our father was greatly esteemed as a young man for his learning; in fact his fame was established throughout the law courts of the province. Subsequently, though he excelled all others in rhetoric, his reputation did not extend beyond Pontus. But he was satisfied with fame in his own land.

"But you," she said, "are renowned in cities and peoples and nations. Churches summon you as an ally and director, and do you not see the grace of God in it all? Do you fail to recognize the cause of such great blessings, that it is your parents' prayers that are lifting you up on high, you that have little or no equipment within yourself for such success?"

Thus she spoke, and I longed for the length of the day to be further extended, that she might never cease delighting our ears with sweetness. But the voice of the choir was summoning us to the evening service, and sending me to church, the great one retired once more to God in prayer. And thus she spent the night.

The Events of the Next Day: Macrina's Last Hours

But when day came it was clear to me from what I saw that the coming day was the utmost limit of her life in the flesh, since the fever consumed all her innate strength. But she, considering the weakness of our minds, was contriving how to divert us from our sorrowful anticipations, and once more with those beautiful words of hers poured out what was left of her suffering soul with short and difficult breathing. Many, indeed, and varied, were the emotions of my heart at what I saw. For nature herself was afflicting me and making me sad; as was only to be expected, since I could no longer hope ever to hear such a voice again. Nor as yet was I reconciled to the thought of losing the common glory of our family, but my mind, as it were inspired by the spectacle, supposed that she would actually rise superior to the common lot. For that she did not even in her last breath find anything strange in the hope of the Resurrection, nor even shrink at the departure from this life, but with lofty mind continued to discuss up to her last breath the convictions she had formed from the beginning about this life—all this seemed to me more than human. Rather did it seem as if some angel had taken human form with a sort of incarnation, to whom it was nothing strange that the mind should remain undisturbed, since he had no kinship or likeness with this life of flesh, and so the flesh did not draw the mind to think on its afflictions.

Therefore[4] I think she revealed to the bystanders that divine and pure love of the invisible bridegroom, which she kept hidden and nourished in the secret places of the soul, and she published abroad the secret disposition of her heart—her hurrying towards Him Whom she desired, that she might speedily be with Him, loosed from the chains of the body. For in very truth her course was directed towards virtue, and nothing else could divert her attention.

Macrina's Dying Prayer

Most of the day had now passed, and the sun was declining towards the West. Her eagerness did not diminish, but as she approached her end, as if she discerned the beauty of the Bridegroom more clearly, she hastened towards the Beloved with the greater eagerness. Such thoughts as these she did not utter, no longer to us who were present, but to Him in person on Whom she gazed fixedly. Her couch had been turned towards the East; and ceasing to converse with us, she spoke henceforward to God in prayer, making supplication with her hands and whispering with a low

---

4   In order to assure them that she was really dying, she uttered aloud the prayer in the next paragraph

voice, so that we could just hear what was said. Such was the prayer; we need not doubt that it reached God and that she, too, was hearing His voice.

"You, O Lord, have freed us from the fear of death. You have made the end of this life the beginning to us of true life. You for a season rest our bodies in sleep and awake them again at the last trumpet. You give our earth, which You have fashioned with Your hands, to the earth to keep in safety. One day You will take again what You have given, transfiguring with immortality and grace our mortal and unsightly remains. You have saved us from the curse and from sin, having become both for our sakes. You have broken the heads of the dragon who had seized us with his jaws, in the yawning gulf of disobedience. You have shown us the way of resurrection, having broken the gates of hell, and brought to nought him who had the power of death—the devil. You have given a sign to those that fear You in the symbol of the Holy Cross, to destroy the adversary and save our life.

"O God eternal, to Whom I have been attached from my mother's womb, Whom my soul has loved with all its strength, to Whom I have dedicated both my flesh and my soul from my youth up until now—do give me an angel of light to conduct me to the place of refreshment, where is the water of rest, in the bosom of the holy Fathers. You that did break the flaming sword and did restore to Paradise the man that was crucified with You and implored Your mercies, remember me, too, in Your Kingdom; because, I, too, was crucified with You, having nailed my flesh to the cross for fear of You, and of Your judgements I have been afraid. Let not the terrible chasm separate me from Your elect. Nor let the Slanderer stand against me in the way; nor let my sin be found before Your eyes, if in anything I have sinned in word or deed or thought, led astray by the weakness of our nature. O You Who have power on earth to forgive sins, forgive me, that I may be refreshed and may be found before You when I put off my body, without defilement on my soul. But may my soul be received into Your hands spotless and undefiled, as an offering before You."

As she said these words she sealed her eyes and mouth and heart with the cross. And gradually her tongue dried up with the fever, she could articulate her words no longer, and her voice died away, and only by the trembling of her lips and the motion of her hands did we recognize that she was praying.

Meanwhile evening had come and a lamp was brought in. All at once she opened the orb of her eyes and looked towards the light, clearly wanting to repeat the thanksgiving sung at the Lighting of the Lamps. But her voice failed and she fulfilled her intention in the heart and by moving her hands, while her lips stirred in sympathy with her inward desire. But when she had finished the thanksgiving, and her hand brought to her face to make the Sign had signified the end of the prayer, she drew a deep breath and closed her life and her prayer together.

Gregory Performs the Last Offices

And now that she was breathless and still, remembering the command that she had given at our first meeting, telling me she wished her hands laid on her eyes, and the accustomed offices done for the body by me, I brought her hands, all numb with disease, on to her holy face, only that I might not seem to neglect her bidding. For her eyes needed none to compose them, being covered gracefully by the lids, just as happens in natural sleep; the lips were suitably closed and the hands lay reverently on the chest, and the whole body had automatically fallen into the right position, and in no way needed the help of the layers-out.

The Sisters' Lament for Their Abbess

Now my mind was becoming unnerved in two ways, from the sight that met my gaze, and the sad wailing of the virgins that sounded in my ears. So far they had remained quiet and suppressed their grief, restraining their impulse to mourn for fear of her, as if they dreaded her rebuke even when her voice was silent, lest in any way a sound should break forth from them contrary to her command and their mistress be grieved in consequence. But when they could no longer subdue their anguish in silence, and grief like some inward fire was smoldering in their hearts, all at once a bitter and irrepressible cry broke out; so that my reason no longer remained calm, but a flood of emotion, like a watercourse in spate, swept it away, and so, neglecting my duties, I gave myself to lamentation. Indeed, the cause for the maidens' weeping seemed to me just and reasonable. For they were not bewailing the loss of human companionship and guidance, nor any other such thing as men grieve over when disaster comes. But it seemed as if they had been torn away from their hope in God and the salvation of their souls, and so they cried and bewailed in this manner—

"The light of our eyes has gone out,

The light that guided our souls has been taken away.

The safety of our life is destroyed,

The seal of immortality is removed,

The bond of restraint has been taken away,

The support of the weak has been broken,

The healing of the sick removed.

In your presence the night became to us as day,

Illumined with pure life,

But now even our day will be turned to gloom."

Saddest of all in their grief were those who called on her as mother and nurse. These were they whom she picked up, exposed by the roadside in the time of famine. She had nursed and reared them, and led them to the pure and stainless life.

But when, as it were from the deep, I recovered my thoughts, I looked towards the holy face and it seemed as if it rebuked me for the confusion of the noisy mourners. So I called to the sisters with a loud voice—"Look at her, and remember her commands, by which she trained you to be orderly and decent in everything. One occasion for tears did this divine soul ordain for us, recommending us to weep at the time of prayer. Which now we may do, by turning the lamentations into psalmody in the same strain."

Vestiana Comes to Help Gregory

I had to shout in order to be heard above the noise of the mourners. Then I besought them to go away for a while to the neighboring house, but asked that some of those whose services she used to welcome when she was alive should stay behind.

Among these was a lady of gentle birth, who had been famous in youth for wealth, good family, physical beauty, and every other distinction. She had married a man of high rank and lived with him a short time. Then, with her body still young, she was released from marriage, and chose the great Macrina as protector and guardian of her widowhood, and spent her time mostly with the virgins, learning from them the life of virtue.

The lady's name was Vestiana, and her father was one of those who composed the council of senators. To her I said that there could be no objection now, at any rate, to putting finer clothing on the body and adorning that pure and stainless form with fair linen clothes. But she said one ought to learn what the saint had thought proper in these matters. For it was not right that anything at all should be done by us contrary to what she would have wished. But just what was dear and pleasing to God, would be her desire also.

Now there was a lady called Lampadia, leader of the band of sisters, a deaconess in rank. She declared that she knew Macrina's wishes in the matter of burial exactly. When I asked her about them (for she happened to be present at our deliberations), she said with tears—

"The saint resolved that a pure life should be her adornment, that this should deck her body in life and her grave in death. But so far as clothes to adorn the body go, she procured none when she was alive, nor did she store them for present purpose. So that not even if we want it will there be anything more than what we have here, since no preparation is made for this need."

"Is it not possible," said I, "to find in the store-cupboard anything to make a fitting funeral?"

"Store-cupboard indeed!" said she, "you have in front of you all her treasure. There is the cloak, there is the head-covering, there the well-worn shoes on the feet. This is all her wealth, these are her riches. There is nothing stored away in secret places beyond what you see, or put away safely in boxes or bedroom. She knew of one store-house alone for her wealth, the treasure in Heaven. There she had stored her all, nothing was left on earth."

"Suppose," said I, "I were to bring some of the things I have got ready for the funeral, should I be doing anything of which she would not have approved?"

"I do not think," said she, "that this would be against her wish. For had she been living, she would have expected such honor from you on two grounds—your priesthood which she always prized so dear, and your relationship, for she would not have repudiated what came to her from her brother. This was why she gave commands that your hands were to prepare her body for burial."

They Find on the Body Marks of Macrina's Sanctity

When we had decided on this, and it was necessary for that sacred body to be robed in linen, we divided the work and applied ourselves to different tasks. I ordered one of my men to bring the robe. But Vestiana above-mentioned was decking that holy head with her own hands, when she put her hand on the neck.

"See," she said, looking at me, "what sort of an ornament has hung on the saint's neck!"

As she spoke, she loosened the fastener behind, then stretched out her hand and showed us the representation of a cross of iron and a ring of the same material, both of which were fastened by a slender thread and rested continually on the heart.

"Let us share the treasure," I said. "You have the phylactery of the cross, I will be content with inheriting the ring."—for the cross had been traced on the seal of this too.

Looking at it, the lady said to me again—"You have made no mistake in choosing this treasure; for the ring is hollow in the hoop, and in it has been hidden a particle of the Cross of Life[5], and so the mark on the seal above shows what is hidden below."

The Story of a Scar

But when it was time that the pure body should be wrapped in its robes, the command of the great departed one made it necessary for me to undertake the ministry; but the sister who shared with me that great inheritance was present and joined in the work.

"Do not let the great wonders accomplished by the saint pass by unnoticed," she remarked, laying bare part of the breast.

"What do you mean?" I said.

"Do you see," she said, "this small faint mark below the neck?" It was like a scar made by a small needle. As she spoke she brought a lamp near to the place she was showing me.

"What is there surprising," I said, "if the body has been branded with some faint mark in this place?"

"This," she replied, "has been left on the body as a token of God's powerful help. For there grew once in this place a cruel disease, and there was a danger either that the

---

5   According to the well-known story, the Cross was discovered by Helena, mother of Constantine the Great (c. 327). The earliest mention of the wood of the Cross as a relic seems to be in Cyril of Jerusalem's *Catechetical Lectures* 4.10, (NPNF² 7), "The whole world has since been filled with pieces of the wood of the cross."

tumor should require an operation, or that the complaint should become quite incurable, if it should spread to the neighborhood of the heart. Her mother implored her often and begged her to receive the attention of a doctor, since the medical art, she said, was sent from God for the saving of men. But she judged it worse than the pain, to uncover any part of the body to a stranger's eyes. So when evening came, after waiting on her mother as usual with her own hands, she went inside the sanctuary and besought the God of healing all night long. A stream of tears fell from her eyes on to the ground, and she used the mud made by the tears as a remedy for her ailment. Then when her mother felt despondent and again urged her to allow the doctor to come, she said it would suffice for the cure of her disease if her mother would make the holy seal on the place with her own hand. But when the mother put her hand within her bosom, to make the sign of the cross on the part, the sign worked and the tumor disappeared."

"But this," she said, "is the tiny trace of it; it appeared then in place of the frightful sore and remained until the end, that it might be, as I imagine, a memorial of the divine visitation, an occasion and reminder of perpetual thanksgiving to God."

When our work came to an end and the body had been decked with the best we had on the spot, the deaconess spoke again, maintaining that it was not fitting that she should be seen by the eyes of the virgins robed like a bride. "But I have," she said, "laid by one of your mother's dark-colored robes which I think would do well laid over her, that this holy beauty be not decked out with the unnecessary splendor of clothing."

Her counsel prevailed, and the robe was laid upon the body. But she was resplendent even in the dark robe, divine power having added, as I think, this final grace to the body, so that, as in the vision of my dream, rays actually seemed to shine forth from her beauty.

The All-Night Vigil: A Crowd of Visitors Arrives

But while we were thus employed and the virgins' voices singing psalms mingled with the lamentations were filling the place, somehow the news had quickly spread throughout the whole neighborhood, and all the people that lived near were streaming towards the place, so that the entrance hall could not longer hold the concourse.

When the all-night vigil for her, accompanied by hymn-singing, as in the case of martyrs' festivals was finished, and the dawn came, the multitude of men and women that had flocked in from all the neighboring country were interrupting the psalms with wailings. But I, sick at heart though I was owing to the calamity, was yet contriving, so far as was possible with what we had, that no suitable accompaniment of such a funeral should be omitted.

Gregory Makes the Funeral Arrangements

I divided the visitors according to sex, and put the crowds of women with the band of virgins, while the men folk I put in the ranks of the monks. I arranged that the psalms should be sung by both sexes in rhythmical and harmonious fashion, as in chorus singing, so that all the voices should blend suitably. But since the day was progressing, and the entire space of the retreat was getting crowded with the multitude of arrivals, the bishop of that district (Araxius by name, who had come with the entire complement of his priests) ordered the funeral procession to start slowly; for there was a long way to go, and the crowd seemed likely to impede brisk movement. At the same time as he gave this order he summoned to him all present who shared with him in the priesthood, that the body might be borne by them.

When this had been settled and his directions were being carried out, I got under the bed and called Araxius to the other side; two other distinguished priests took the hinder part of the bed. Then I went forward, slowly as to be expected, our progress being but gradual. For the people thronged round the bed and all were insatiable to see that holy sight, so that it was not easy for us to complete our journey. On either side we were flanked by a considerable number of deacons and servants, escorting the bier in order, all holding wax tapers.

The whole thing resembled a mystic procession, and from beginning to end the voices blended in singing psalms, that, for example, that comes in the Hymn of the Three Children. Seven or eight stades intervened between the Retreat and the abode of the Holy Martyrs, in which also the bodies of our parents were laid. With difficulty did we accomplish the journey in the best part of a day, for the crowds that came with us and those that were constantly joining us did not allow our progress to be what we wished.

Arrival At The Church: The Burial Service

But when we got inside the church we laid down the bed and turned first to prayer. But our prayer was the signal for the people's lamentation to start again. For when the voice of psalmody was still, and the virgins gazed on the holy face, and the grave of our parents was already being opened, in which it had been decided that Macrina should be laid, a woman cried out impulsively that after this hour we should see that divine face no more. Then the rest of the virgins cried out the same, and a disorderly confusion disturbed the orderly and solemn chanting of psalms, all being upset at the wailing of the virgins. With difficulty did we succeed in procuring silence by our gesture, and the precentor taking the lead and intoning the accustomed prayers of the Church, the people composed themselves at last to prayer.

The Family Grave is Opened

When the prayer had come to its due close, fear entered my mind of transgressing the divine command, which forbids us to uncover the shame of father or mother. "And how," said I, "shall I escape such condemnation if I gaze at the common shame of human nature made manifest in the bodies of my parents? Since they are all decayed and dissolved, as must be expected, and turned into foul and repulsive shapelessness."

As I thought of these things and the anger of Noah against his son was striking fear into me, the story of Noah advised me what was to be done. Before the lid of the grave was lifted sufficiently to reveal the bodies to our gaze, they were covered by a pure linen cloth stretched across from each end. And now that the bodies were hidden under the cloth, we—myself, that is, and the aforementioned bishop of the district—took up that holy body from the bed and laid it down by the side of the mother, thus fulfilling the common prayer of both. For both were with one voice asking God for this boon all their lives long, that their bodies should be mingled with one another after death, and their comradeship in life should not even in death be broken.

The Funeral Over, Gregory Returns Home

But when we had completed all the accustomed funeral rites, and it became necessary to return home, I first threw myself on the grave and embraced the dust, and then I started on my way back, downcast and tearful, pondering over the greatness of my loss.

On my way I met a distinguished soldier who had a military command in a little city of Pontus named Sebastopolis, and dwelt there with his subordinates. He met me in friendly fashion when I reached the town, and was greatly disturbed to hear of the calamity, for he was linked to us by ties both of relationship and friendship. He told me a story of a marvelous episode in her life, which I shall incorporate into my history and then close my tale. When we had ceased our tears and had entered into conversation, he said to me—"Learn what manner of goodness has been taken away from human life." With this prelude he began his narrative.

The Soldier's Story

"My wife and I once had an earnest desire to pay a visit to the school of virtue. For so I think the place ought to be called, in which that blessed soul had her abode. Now there lived with us also our little daughter, who had been left with an affliction of the eye after an infectious illness. And her appearance was hideous and pitiable, the membrane round the eye being enlarged and whitish from the complaint. But when we came inside that divine abode, my wife and I separated in our visit to those seekers after philosophy according to our sex. I went to the men's department, presided over by Peter, your brother; while my wife went to the women's side and conversed with the saint. And when a suitable interval had elapsed, we considered it time to depart from the Retreat, and already our preparations were being made for this, but kind protests were raised from both sides equally. Your brother was urging me to stay and partake of the philosopher's table; and the blessed lady would not let my wife go, but holding our little girl in her bosom, said she would not give her up before she had prepared a meal for them and entertained them with the riches of philosophy. And kissing the child, as was natural, and putting her lips to her eyes, she saw the complaint of the pupil and said—

"'If you grant me this favor and share our meal, I will give you in return a reward not unworthy of such an honor.'

"'What is that?' said the child's mother.

"'I have a drug,' said the great lady, 'which is powerful to cure eye complaints.'

"And then news was brought me from the women's apartments, telling me of this promise, and we gladly remained, thinking little of the pressing necessity of starting on our journey.

"But when the feast came to an end and we had said the prayer, great Peter waiting on us with his own hands and cheering us, and when holy Macrina had dismissed my wife with all courtesy, then at last we went home together with glad and cheerful hearts, telling one another as we journeyed what had befallen us. I described to her what had happened in the men's room, both what I had heard and seen. She told of every detail as in a history, and thought nothing ought to be left out, even the smallest points. She told everything in order, keeping the sequence of the narrative. When she came to the point at which the promise was made to cure the child's eyes, she broke off her tale.

"'Oh, what have we done?' she cried. 'How could we have neglected the promise, that salve-cure that the lady said she would give?'

"I was vexed at the carelessness, and bade someone run

back quickly to fetch it. Just as this was being done, the child, who was in her nurse's arms, looked at her mother, and the mother looked at the child eyes.

"'Stop,' she said, 'being vexed at the carelessness,'—she cried aloud with joy and fright. 'For, see! Nothing of what was promised to us is lacking! She has indeed given her the true drug which cures disease; it is the healing that comes from prayer. She has both given it and it has already proved efficacious, and nothing is left of the affliction of the eye. It is all purged away by that divine drug.'

"And as she said this, she took up the child and laid her in my arms, And I understood the marvels of the Gospel that hitherto had been incredible to me and said—

"'What is there surprising in the blind recovering their sight by the hand of God, when now His handmaiden, accomplishing those cures by faith in Him, has worked a thing not much inferior to those miracles?'"

Such was his story; it was interrupted by sobs, and tears choked his utterance. So much for the soldier and his tale.

Conclusion

I do not think it advisable to add to my narrative all the similar things that we heard from those who lived with her and knew her life accurately. For most men judge what is credible in the way of a tale by the measure of their own experience. But what exceeds the capacity of the hearer, men receive with insult and suspicion of falsehood, as remote from truth. Consequently I omit that extraordinary agricultural operation in the famine time, how that the corn for the relief of need, though constantly distributed, suffered no perceptible diminution, remaining always in bulk the same as before it was distributed to the needs of the suppliants. And after this there are happenings still more surprising, of which I might tell. Healings of diseases, and castings of demons, and true predictions of the future. All are believed to be true, even though apparently incredible, by those who have investigated them accurately.

But by the carnally minded they are judged outside the possible. Those, I mean, who do not know that according to the proportion of faith so is given the distribution of spiritual gifts, little to those of little faith, much to those who have plenty of "sea-room" in their religion.

And so, lest the unbeliever should be injured by being led to disbelieve the gifts of God, I have abstained from a consecutive narrative of these sublime wonders, thinking it sufficient to conclude my life of Macrina with what has been already said.

THE END